REAL ESTATE
Exam PREP

WASHINGTON

Dearborn
Real Estate Education

While a great deal of care has been taken to provide accurate and current information, the ideas, suggestions, general principles, and conclusions presented in this text are subject to local, state and federal laws and regulations, court cases, and any revisions of same. The reader is urged to consult legal counsel regarding any points of law. This publication should not be used as a substitute for competent legal advice.

Publisher: Evan M. Butterfield
Development Editor: Amanda Rahn
Development Editor: David Cirillo
Associate Development Editor: Michael J. Scafuri
Production Manager: Bryan Samolinski
Creative Director: Lucy Jenkins
Cover Design: Gail Chandler

Testbank Reviewer: Susan Davis
Exam Prep Series Content Consultant: Marie Spodek, DREI

Introduction

Welcome to *Washington Exam Prep*! When you bought this book, you showed that you are serious about passing the exam and getting your real estate license. This is *NOT* an easy test. For people whose test-taking skills are weak, or who haven't adequately prepared, the exam can be a nightmare. For those who have taken the time and effort to study and review, however, the exam can be a much more positive experience.

It's pretty obvious, though, that if you practice and review key material, your test score will improve. This book is your key to exam success.

The process is simple: Just work your way through the practice questions, taking your time and answering each one carefully. Then check your answers by studying the Answer Key, where you'll find both the correct answer to each question as well as an explanation of *why* that answer is correct. It might be a good idea to review your classroom materials and textbook before you start.

Remember: These 203 questions reflect as closely as possible the topic coverage of the state-specific portion of your exam only! For the balance of the test, you'll need to use a "national" exam prep book. And remember, too, that it takes study and hard work on your part to pass the licensing exam: no single study aid will do the trick alone.

Experts who are familiar with the Washington licensing examination, as well as real estate law and practice, prepared this book. You've taken the first step toward your success as a real estate professional: Good Luck!

Dearborn Real Estate Education

1. A licensed broker procures a ready, willing and able buyer for his or her seller-principal. The seller first accepts the buyer's offer in writing, then experiences a change of heart and withdraws the original acceptance. In this situation, the broker

   A. is entitled to collect a commission.
   B. is out of luck because the transaction was never completed.
   C. may sue the buyer.
   D. may retain the deposit as a commission.

2. A real estate company has entered into agency agreements with both a seller and a buyer. The buyer is interested in making an offer on the seller's property. Can this occur?

   A. No, the real estate company would then be a dual agent.
   B. Yes, as long as written agency agreements have been entered into with both parties.
   C. Yes, if Seller has agreed to pay the commission.
   D. Yes, if both Buyer and Seller give their consent to dual agency.

3. The listing agreement with a seller has expired, and the seller lists with a different brokerage firm. The original listing agent now has a buyer interested in the seller's property. The original listing agent

   A. is a dual agent.
   B. cannot disclose to the buyer offers received on the seller's property while it was listed with him.
   C. cannot disclose to the buyer information about the physical condition of the property.
   D. cannot represent the buyer.

4. A real estate salesperson has been working with buyers. After helping them negotiate for their dream home, the buyers ask the salesperson if she can help them secure a mortgage. The salesperson knows a lender that pays a fee for referring purchasers to them. Should the salesperson refer the buyers to this lender?

   A. No, this would be an unwise referral.
   B. Yes, if the salesperson and the buyers have previously entered into a written buyer agency agreement.
   C. Yes, if the salesperson discloses the referral fee to the sellers.
   D. Yes, if the lender offers the best interest rates and terms available in the market.

5. The presumption now exists in Washington that the licensee represents the

   A. buyer.
   B. seller.
   C. both the buyer and the seller.
   D. neither the buyer nor the seller.

6. A buyer prospect is interested in seeing a house listed with a real estate company, but does not wish to enter into a buyer agency agreement. A salesperson from the real estate company can show the buyer an in-house listing if the

   A. salesperson obtains the seller's permission.
   B. buyer verbally agrees to buyer agency.
   C. salesperson provides the buyer with an agency disclosure that the real estate company represents the seller.
   D. salesperson provides the buyer with a dual agency consent form.

7. Two separate salespeople from the same brokerage wish to represent different parties in the same transaction, i.e., one represents the seller, the other the buyer. Is this legal in Washington?

    A. Only one agent from a brokerage may be involved in a transaction at any given time.
    B. If the broker permits this, the broker is breaking the law and is subject to fines, imprisonment, or both.
    C. Each salesperson represents only the party with whom he or she has an agency relationship.
    D. Both salespeople are presumed to represent both parties as dual agents.

8. Buyer-agent contracts in Washington

    A. must be in writing to be enforceable.
    B. must be on specific forms.
    C. are not regulated under the license laws.
    D. are not necessary.

9. In Washington, confidential information concerning a principal may not be disclosed. However, some information must be disclosed. Of the following, which information must be disclosed?

    A. Information that was acquired by the licensee during the course of an agency relationship with the principal
    B. Information that the principal reasonably expects to be kept confidential.
    C. That which relates to material facts about the property
    D. Information which, if disclosed, would operate to the detriment of the principal

10. Washington State agency law was designed to

    A. confuse the public and create more paperwork.
    B. eliminate vicarious liability and imputed knowledge as to consumers.
    C. increase instances of dual agency to help agents make more money.
    D. move away from presumed agency relationships.

11. In a dual agency situation, a broker may collect a commission from both the seller and the buyer if

    A. the broker holds a state license.
    B. the buyer and the seller are related by blood or marriage.
    C. both parties give their informed consent to the dual compensation.
    D. both parties are represented by attorneys.

12. The licensee must provide a pamphlet on the law of real estate to all parties to whom he or she renders brokerage services prior to which of the following events?

    A. Party signs an agency agreement
    B. Party signs an offer in a real estate transaction handled by the licensee
    C. Party consents to dual agency
    D. Any of these

13. A buyer should consider the disclosure statement to be a

    A. warranty by the seller of the condition of the property.
    B. partial agreement between the buyer and the seller.
    C. disclosure statement only.
    D. guaranty that every problem has been disclosed.

14. Sellers of which of the following are obligated to make a property disclosure?

    A. Investment property
    B. Multi-family property
    C. Residential property
    D. Commercial property

15. The property disclosure law applies to a

    A. foreclosure.
    B. deed-in-lieu of foreclosure.
    C. sale by a lien holder who acquired the property through foreclosure or deed-in-lieu of foreclosure.
    D. sale of a duplex.

16. The property disclosure law applies to a gift or other transfer to a

    A. child of any parent or spouse of a transferor.
    B. parent of a transferor.
    C. friend or acquaintance of a transferor.
    D. spouse of a transferor.

17. A buyer and seller enter into a written contract to sell/purchase. When is the last possible moment that the disclosure statement may be delivered to the buyer?

    A. At least five business days before contract offer and acceptance
    B. No later than five business days after contract offer and acceptance
    C. At the time of contract signing
    D. At least 48 hours before contract offer and acceptance

18. Five years ago, Unit 5B in a condominium community was the site of a brutal and highly publicized murder. The unit was sold to an elderly woman who contracted the AIDS virus in a blood transfusion and died in the unit last year. As the agent for the woman's estate, what are your disclosure responsibilities to prospective purchasers of Unit 5B?

    A. You must disclose both the murder and the AIDS-related death.
    B. You are specifically prohibited by law from disclosing either event.
    C. You are specifically relieved of liability for nondisclosure of either event.
    D. You do not need to disclose the murder, but you must disclose the AIDS-related death.

19. A broker took a listing for a small office building. Because the property is in excellent condition and produces a good, steady income, the broker's salesperson has decided to purchase it as an investment. If the broker's salesperson wishes to buy this property, the salesperson must

    A. resign as the broker's agent and make an offer after the owner has retained another broker.
    B. have some third party purchase the property on the salesperson's behalf so that the owner does not learn the true identity of the purchaser.
    C. obtain permission from the Washington Real Estate Commission
    D. inform the owner in writing that the salesperson is a licensee before making an offer.

20. Six months after the buyer bought a house, the roof leaked during a rainstorm. When the house was listed, the seller told the broker that the roof leaked, but they agreed not to tell any prospective buyers. The broker, who is the sellers' agent, claims that the buyer did not ask about the roof. Under these facts the buyer

    A. can sue the broker for non-disclosure.
    B. cannot sue the broker under the license law.
    C. can sue the seller under license law.
    D. cannot do anything because the leaking roof could have been discovered by inspection.

21. A real estate licensee must give the Agency Disclosure Statement to prospective purchasers/tenants

    A. before they are shown any properties.
    B. at an open house.
    C. at the closing table.
    D. before any offers to purchase or lease are signed by the purchasers/tenants.

22. A real estate licensee has signed a brokerage agreement with a tenant who is looking for an apartment to rent. The licensee does not charge a fee to prospective tenants; rather, the licensee receives a commission from landlords. The licensee tells a landlord that the prospective tenant could probably pay a somewhat higher rent than the landlord is asking. Which of the following statements is true?

    A. The licensee owes the statutory agency duties to the landlord who pays the commission.
    B. The licensee's disclosure to the landlord was appropriate under these circumstances.
    C. The licensee's disclosure violated the statutory duties owed to the tenant.
    D. Because the licensee is not charging a fee to prospective tenants, the licensee has violated Washington agency statute.

23. The property disclosure law does not apply to a transfer in which a buyer had an ownership interest in the property

    A. for a period of not more than three years prior to the date of the transfer.
    B. within two years of the date of the transfer.
    C. for a period of not less than two years prior to the date of the transfer.
    D. at any time prior to the date of the transfer.

24. In a "split" or "designated" agency transaction, who is actually considered a dual agent?

    A. The broker
    B. Salesperson who represents the buyer
    C. Salesperson that represents the seller
    D. No one, the broker is considered a facilitator

25. A real estate broker representing the seller knows that the property has a cracked foundation and that its former owner committed suicide in the kitchen. The broker must disclose

    A. both facts.
    B. the suicide, but not the foundation.
    C. the cracked foundation, but disclosing the suicide could constitute a breach of duty to the client.
    D. neither fact.

26. A Washington broker has entered into a listing agreement with the seller. Another broker, who has been working with a buyer, learns of the property through the MLS. Typically the second, cooperating broker would represent the

    A. seller as a subagent.
    B. buyer as an agent.
    C. buyer as a subagent.
    D. neither buyer nor seller.

27. When a broker represents the seller of real estate, an agency disclosure must be given to the

    A. seller, at the beginning of the first personal meeting with the seller concerning the real estate.
    B. seller, at the time the listing agreement is signed.
    C. purchaser, before the purchase and sale contract is signed.
    D. purchaser, at the beginning of the first personal meeting with the purchaser.

28. The Realty Company has entered into agency agreements with both a seller and a buyer. The seller and the buyer have signed the Dual Agency Consent Agreement. The salesperson with The Realty Company has been working with the buyer. Legally, the salesperson may

    A. provide comparable market data to the seller, after the buyer requests and receives such data from the salesperson.
    B. give the buyer's financial qualifications to the seller.
    C. inform the buyer that the seller will accept less than the listing price.
    D. disclose to the seller that the buyer will pay more than the offering price.

29. A brokerage's relationship with a buyer or seller as agent, non-agent facilitator, or dual agent must be determined, and all necessary agreements executed

    A. at any time after a purchase and sale agreement is executed by the parties.
    B. at the time of the first substantial business contact.
    C. no later than the time a purchase and sale agreement is prepared.
    D. no later than the closing.

30. A buyer who is a client of the broker wants to purchase a house that the broker has listed for sale. Which of the following statements is true?

    A. If the listing salesperson and selling salesperson are two different people, there is no problem.
    B. The broker should refer the buyer to another broker to negotiate the sale.
    C. The seller and buyer must be informed of the situation and agree in writing to the broker representing both of them.
    D. The buyer should not have been shown a house listed by the broker.

31. The Real Estate Brokerage Agency Law requires that the licensee do all of the following EXCEPT

    A. keep confidential all confidential information that the seller has provided.
    B. advise the seller to seek expert advice on matters relating to the transaction that are beyond the agent's expertise.
    C. disclose all existing material facts known by the licensee that might affect the sale and are not apparent or readily ascertainable to a potential purchaser.
    D. conduct a property inspection.

32. In Washington, the real estate license law is administered by the

    A. Washington Real Estate Commission.
    B. Washington State Department of Licensing.
    C. Washington Association of REALTORS®.
    D. Washington State Department of Records.

33. How are members of the Washington Real Estate Commission selected?

    A. By the governor
    B. Public election
    C. By the state Association of REALTORS®
    D. Elected by real estate licensees

34. The director of the Department of Licensing has the authority to

    A. institute a program of real estate education.
    B. hold educational conferences for the benefit of the industry.
    C. administer the exams given at the testing sites.
    D. prepare the real estate exam.

35. The real estate license law consists of

    A. laws passed by the state legislature.
    B. rules promulgated by the director of the Department of Licensing.
    C. both laws and rules.
    D. laws, rules, and common law as expressed through court decisions.

36. All real estate license fees are paid to the

    A. state auditor and placed in the general fund for real estate taxes for that county.
    B. state treasurer and placed in the public services fund of the state treasury.
    C. state treasurer and placed in the real estate commission account in the state treasury.
    D. Washington Real Estate Commission and placed in the real estate recovery fund.

37. A license is issued to a corporation, limited liability company, or limited liability partnership. Who is entitled to act as a real estate broker?

    A. All corporate officers, managers, and partners
    B. One corporate officer, manager or partner who is named in the license application
    C. All individuals hired by the corporation or partnership for the express purpose of conducting real estate business
    D. Any individual acting on behalf of the corporation or partnership

38. An individual may legally serve in which of the following capacities without a real estate license?

    A. Real estate broker
    B. Associate broker
    C. Real Estate salesperson
    D. None of the above

39. Under Washington Licensing law, a partnership, association, or corporation will be granted a license only if

    A. an officer, partner, or manager is designated as the broker.
    B. every member and officer actively participating in the brokerage business has a broker license.
    C. all papers are filed with the Secretary of State.
    D. the brokerage business has paid a one-time fee to the guaranty fund.

40. "Engaging in the real estate business" consists of acting for another and for a fee in all of the following activities EXCEPT

    A. managing real estate.
    B. selling a new manufactured or mobile home.
    C. selling real estate.
    D. collecting rent for the use of real estate.

41. Which of the following is a requirement for obtaining a broker's license?

    A. Being 21 years of age or older
    B. Having a high school diploma or its equivalent
    C. Having a bachelor's degree in real estate
    D. Having at least three years of experience as a salesperson previous to applying for the broker's license examination

42. A broker may establish one or more branch offices under a name or names different from that of the main office with the approval of the director only if

    A. the broker's time is split equally between the main office and the branch office.
    B. the branch office is located no more than five miles from the main office.
    C. there are at least five licensed real estate licensees working full time at each branch office.
    D. each branch office is clearly identified as a branch or division of the main office.

43. In Washington, a broker's license can be issued to any of the following EXCEPT

 A. an individual.
 B. a corporation.
 C. a partnership.
 D. a trust.

44. In Washington, one of the requirements for obtaining a broker's license is having successfully completed at least 120 hours of instruction in real estate. Three 30-hour courses are mandatory. Which of the following could be used as an elective?

 A. Trust Accounts
 B. Real Estate Law
 C. Business Management
 D. Brokerage Management

45. A person successfully completed her real estate education requirement on November 1, 2001. What is the latest date on which she may apply for a salesperson's license?

 A. December 31, 2004
 B. May 31, 2002
 C. October 31, 2005
 D. October 31, 2006

46. If a broker applicant receives an experience waiver and then fails to pass the broker's examination, the applicant

 A. may retake the examination once before losing the privilege of the waiver.
 B. loses the privilege of the waiver and must then satisfy the two-year experience requirement.
 C. must take additional coursework in lieu of the experience requirement.
 D. may retake the examination twice before losing the privilege of the waiver.

47. When obtaining a broker's license, which of the following may not be used as an experience waiver in lieu of the required two years experience as a salesperson?

 A. Five years experience as an officer of a bank, title, or mortgage company, involving all phases of real estate transactions
 B. Experience as an attorney at law with practice in real estate transactions for not less than one year
 C. Post-secondary education with minor study in real estate for four years
 D. Post-secondary education with major study in real estate together with one-year experience as a real estate salesperson

48. When the director receives a statement or accusation concerning a licensee, the director will

 A. place the statement or accusation in the licensee's file until the licensee has three such accusations, then investigate.
 B. carry out a preliminary investigation of the facts to determine whether formal action is warranted.
 C. immediately carry out a full, formal investigation of the accused.
 D. give the licensee a preliminary warning, including a statement that further accusations will result in a license suspension.

49. A copy of the order setting the time and place of a disciplinary hearing and a copy of the verified statement of accusation against the licensee must be given to the licensee prior to the hearing. The advance notice must be given at least

    A. 7 days before the day of the hearing.
    B. 10 days before the day of the hearing.
    C. 20 days before the day of the hearing.
    D. 30 days before the day of the hearing.

50. A disciplinary hearing will be conducted by

    A. a federal judge.
    B. a municipal judge.
    C. the director of the Department of Licensing or an Administrative Law Judge.
    D. the director of the Department of Licensing or a Circuit Court Judge.

51. If the director determines that the evidence supports the accusation against a licensee by a preponderance of evidence, the director

    A. may impose sanctions.
    B. must initiate a full investigation.
    C. is required to suspend the individual's license.
    D. is required to revoke the individual's license.

52. The licensee wishes to appeal the decision made by the director in a disciplinary hearing. To file an appeal, what must the licensee post with the court clerk?

    A. $50 filing fee
    B. $100 filing fee
    C. $500 bond
    D. $1000 bond

53. Any violation of the license law is a gross misdemeanor and can be prosecuted by the

    A. county prosecutor or the state attorney general.
    B. district attorney.
    C. county prosecutor.
    D. state attorney general.

54. After notice and hearing and a determination that a person has violated a provision of the License Law or a lawful order or rule of the director, the director may issue that person a

    A. restricted license.
    B. cease and desist order.
    C. pending violation procedure.
    D. fine or imprisonment.

55. A temporary cease and desist order is served. Unless the licensee requests a later hearing, the hearing to determine whether the order becomes permanent is held within

    A. 60 days after the department receives the request for hearing.
    B. 90 days after the department receives the request for hearing.
    C. 30 days after the department receives the request for hearing.
    D. 10 days after the department receives the request for hearing.

56. If the licensee continues to sell any real estate where the interests of the public are endangered, disciplinary sanctions are warranted after who has stated the objections?

    A. Principal
    B. Director
    C. Real estate commission
    D. EPA

57. Disciplinary sanctions are warranted if the licensee engages in blind advertising. Blind advertising is advertising that does not include

    A. the cost of the property.
    B. all known material facts concerning the property.
    C. the broker's name as licensed.
    D. the address of the property.

58. If a corporation that has been incorporated in another state applies for a real estate license, the applicant must furnish

    A. a certified copy of certificate of authority to conduct business in the state of Washington.
    B. a list of its salespeople but not its officers and directors.
    C. proof of three years of real estate activity.
    D. the license number of each of the salespeople in the other state.

59. In order to take the real estate examination, the applicant must do all of the following EXCEPT

    A. apply on the prescribed form and pay the license exam fee.
    B. provide a parent's signature.
    C. provide proof of honesty, truthfulness, and good reputation.
    D. provide proof of identity, which may include fingerprints.

60. If an applicant passes the licensing examination, he or she has how long to become licensed before the exam must be retaken?

    A. One year
    B. Five years
    C. Eighteen months
    D. Two years

61. To get a salesperson or associate broker license, the license application must be signed by the

    A. executive officer of the local REALTORS® Association.
    B. salesperson or associate broker who is applying for the license.
    C. broker or designated broker to whom the license will be issued.
    D. school administrator who provided the course work.

62. What is the minimum passing score on both the state and national portions of the real estate salesperson examination?

    A. 70%
    B. 75%
    C. 80%
    D. 85%

63. Persons who have been convicted of a crime within ten years of applying for a real estate license may be required to submit

    A. to periodic drug analysis.
    B. fingerprint identification.
    C. a semi-annual statement of conduct.
    D. to supervision by the office of corrections for each county in which he or she will be conducting business.

64. An applicant has passed the licensing exam and submitted the completed license application form and fee. The applicant may begin working as a real estate licensee using the completed license application as an interim license. This interim license is effective for up to

    A. 45 days.
    B. 60 days.
    C. 30 days.
    D. 90 days.

65. Which of the following individuals or entities may receive an interim license?

    A. Designated brokers for corporations
    B. Limited liability companies
    C. Partnerships and limited liability partnerships
    D. Salesperson who sent in her application

66. When do real estate licenses issued to individuals expire?

    A. On the applicant's first birthday following issuance of the license
    B. On the applicant's second birthday following issuance of the license
    C. One year from the date of the issuance of the license
    D. Two years from the date of the issuance of the license

67. When must licenses be renewed?

    A. At least two weeks before the expiration date
    B. They do not need to be renewed unless previously revoked
    C. No more than 24 hours after the expiration date
    D. On or before the expiration date

68. If a year passes after the expiration date of a real estate license, the

    A. individual must pay a fee to get the license reinstated.
    B. license will be cancelled.
    C. applicant must write a letter to the director requesting the reinstatement of his or her license.
    D. individual must take one continuing education course of 30 hours from an approved school of his or her choice.

69. In order to renew their licenses after the first renewal, all real estate licensees must complete approved real estate courses for a total of

    A. 30 clock-hours of instruction every two years.
    B. 30 clock-hours of instruction every four years.
    C. 60 clock-hours of instruction every two years
    D. 30 clock-hours of instruction every year.

70. If a licensee takes more than the required thirty hours of instruction in real estate courses within two years,

    A. all additional hours of instruction may be carried toward credit in a subsequent two-year period.
    B. up to 10 hours of instruction may be carried toward credit in a subsequent two-year period.
    C. up to 15 hours of instruction may be carried toward credit in a subsequent two-year period.
    D. the additional hours of instruction cannot be used toward credit in any subsequent renewal period.

71. In Washington, all of the following would be grounds for revoking a broker's license EXCEPT

    A. being convicted of a felony in a court of competent jurisdiction.
    B. advertising in a newspaper that he or she is a member of the National Association of Real Estate when in fact he or she is not.
    C. depositing escrow money in his or her personal checking account.
    D. agreeing with a seller to accept a listing for more than the normal commission rate.

72. The real estate commission has the power to revoke a salesperson's license if the salesperson

    A. keeps records relating to a real estate transaction for a period of only three years following consummation of that transaction.
    B. attempts to represent a buyer.
    C. enters into an exclusive listing contract.
    D. deposits a buyer's down payment in her own bank account.

73. In Washington, a broker may have his or her license suspended or revoked for all of the following actions EXCEPT

    A. misrepresenting his or her membership in any state or national real estate association.
    B. depositing earnest money into the firm's escrow account.
    C. acting as a vehicle dealer without having a license to do so.
    D. advertising in any manner without affixing the licensed broker's name.

74. Which of the following actions are legal and not a violation of license law?

    A. Encouraging a seller to reject an offer because the prospective buyer is a Methodist
    B. Placing a "For Sale" sign in front of a house after asking the seller's permission and receiving written permission to go ahead
    C. Advertising that individuals who attend a promotional presentation will receive a prize without mentioning that they will also have to take a day trip to a new subdivision site
    D. A real estate salesperson accepting a referral fee from an out-of-state broker

75. If a broker tells a lender that the sales price on a property is something above its actual sales price in order to assist the buyer in obtaining a larger loan, the

    A. broker has done nothing wrong as long as the appraisal substantiates this price.
    B. buyer is likely to receive an interest rate break.
    C. broker can lose his or her license and be fined.
    D. buyer can receive a higher mortgage amount.

76. Salesperson J-H placed the following order with the telephone company: List my name in the directory under the heading, Real Estate, as "J-H, Real Estate Salesperson, Residential Property My Specialty." J-H is also required to include

    A. her license number.
    B. the expiration date of her license.
    C. her street address.
    D. the name of her employing broker.

77. If a person lawfully relies on the word, representation, or conduct of a licensee who knowingly commits or is a party to any material fraud, misrepresentation, concealment, conspiracy, collusion, trick, scheme, or device, who is subject to disciplinary sanctions?

    A. Only the licensee
    B. Any party involved in the misconduct
    C. The principal
    D. All of the above

78. When advertising real property, real estate licensees

    A. may state only the licensee's box number or street address.
    B. may simply give a telephone number to call for more information.
    C. must indicate that the ads were placed in the name of a licensed real estate broker.
    D. must identify the owner of the property.

79. A real estate salesperson decides to sell his or her own property without using a broker. When advertising the property, the salesperson

    A. must disclose the name, address and phone number of his employing broker.
    B. must disclose the fact that she or he is a real estate licensee.
    C. if acting as a private citizen, does not need to disclose licensed status.
    D. is prohibited from selling his or her own home in this manner by license law.

80. A licensee must turn over money or documents upon demand within

    A. 5 days.
    B. 30 days.
    C. 45 days.
    D. 60 days.

81. A salesperson has developed a website on the Internet. What, if anything, must the salesperson include?

    A. The licensee's name and the firm's name as registered with the regulatory agency of the jurisdiction that licensed it to do business
    B. The broker's license number
    C. A list of all licensed salespersons in the office
    D. There is no need for additional disclosures

82. Licensees who own/maintain individual websites should be careful to do all the following EXCEPT

    A. ensure that when listings have expired they are removed from websites in a timely manner.
    B. periodically review the advertising and marketing information on their website.
    C. selectively post and advertise other licensed entities listings.
    D. avoid giving the impression that he or she is licensed or is providing services in jurisdictions where a license in not held.

83. A personal assistant working under the direct instruction and supervision of a licensee must hold a license if he or she

    A. greets people at an open house or model unit and distributes preprinted promotional literature.
    B. answers questions and interprets printed information concerning the property.
    C. performs clerical duties such as typing, answering the phone, forwarding calls, and scheduling appointments for licensees.
    D. submits forms and changes to multiple listing services or obtains status reports on loan progress and credit reports.

84. In Washington, real estate commissions are

    A. set by law.
    B. fixed by the Washington Real Estate Commission.
    C. determined by local groups of brokers.
    D. negotiable between the seller and buyer and broker.

85. Commissions earned by a broker in a real estate transaction

    A. are determined by agreement of the broker and his or her principal.
    B. may be shared with an unlicensed person as a referral fee, provided that such person aided the broker in bringing the buyer and seller together.
    C. may be deducted from the earnest money deposit and claimed by the broker as soon as the buyer and seller execute the purchase and sales agreement.
    D. are based on a schedule of commission rates set by the Washington Real Estate Commission.

86. All funds received by a broker on behalf of his or her principal must be deposited in an escrow or trust account

    A. within three days of receiving the offer.
    B. within three days of obtaining all signatures for the contract.
    C. no later than five working days after receiving the offer.
    D. no later than the first banking day following receipt of the funds.

87. A broker received an earnest money deposit from a buyer. Under Washington law, the broker should

    A. open a special, separate escrow account that will contain funds for this transaction only.
    B. deposit the money in an existing interest-bearing escrow account in which all earnest money received from buyers may be held at the same time.
    C. immediately (or by the next business day) deposit the earnest money in the broker's personal interest-bearing checking or savings account.
    D. hold the earnest money deposit in a secure place in the broker's real estate brokerage office until the offer is accepted.

88. The broker received a buyer's earnest money check for $5,000 and immediately cashed it. At closing, the broker handed the seller a personal check drawn on the broker's own bank account for $5,300, representing the original earnest money plus 6 percent interest. The broker

    A. should have deposited the money in a special non-interest-bearing bank account.
    B. properly cashed the check, but should have kept the interest.
    C. should have deposited the money in his personal bank account, and would have been entitled to keep the interest as a service fee.
    D. should have deposited the money in a special bank account, and should have discussed the interest with the parties.

89. The individual responsible for the custody, safety, and correctness of the entries of all required real estate records within a brokerage firm is the

    A. office manager.
    B. broker.
    C. secretary or other individual assigned to maintain the records.
    D. salesperson or associate broker who must maintain the records for those transactions with which he or she is involved.

90. The broker is required to keep all of the following bank trust account records EXCEPT

    A. a client's accounting ledger summarizing all moneys received and all moneys disbursed for each transaction or each account.
    B. separate ledger sheets, in conjunction with client ledgers, for each tenant (including security deposit), lessee, vendee, or mortgagor.
    C. a duplicate cash receipts journal that is kept in a safe deposit box.
    D. reconciled bank statements and cancelled checks for all trust bank accounts.

91. The broker must keep pre-numbered checks with the check register and

    A. non-validated, duplicate bank deposit slips.
    B. cash disbursements journal or check stubs.
    C. a duplicate receipt book in a safe deposit box.
    D. statements that have not been reconciled.

92. The broker must keep validated duplicate bank deposit slips and

    A. a duplicate receipt book or a cash receipts journal recording all receipts.
    B. photocopied checks.
    C. how commissions for salespersons were calculated.
    D. detailed interview records.

93. For each transaction, the broker must maintain a transaction folder containing all of the following EXCEPT

    A. agreements and documents.
    B. closing statements and correspondence.
    C. leases.
    D. deeds.

94. A lending institution may use an individual's marital status to make which of the following determinations?

    A. Restricting the amount or use of credit extended or imposing different terms or conditions with respect to the credit extended
    B. Denying credit to the individual
    C. Increasing the charges, fees, or collateral required to secure any credit extended to the individual
    D. None of these determinations may be based on marital status.

95. The Law Against Discrimination is administered by the

    A. Washington State Human Rights Commission.
    B. Equal Credit Opportunity Council.
    C. Americans with Disabilities Council.
    D. Department of Housing and Urban Development.

96. If a seller does not know the answer to a question on the property disclosure form, he or she should

    A. leave the space blank.
    B. put a bold black line through the space.
    C. enter an answer that is likely to be correct.
    D. enter "don't know."

97. Unless otherwise agreed to, within three business days of receipt of the real property transfer disclosure statement, the buyer may

    A. approve and accept the real property disclosure statement.
    B. rescind the agreement for the purchase and sale of the property.
    C. either approve or rescind the agreement.
    D. do only what is explicitly written in the purchase agreement.

98. Concerning the required Real Property Transfer Disclosure Statement, if the buyer does not deliver a written rescission notice to the seller within the three-day period, the

    A. buyer forfeits his or her opportunity to buy the property.
    B. real property disclosure statement will be deemed approved and accepted by the buyer.
    C. seller can sue the buyer for damages.
    D. real property transfer disclosure statement will be deemed rejected by the buyer.

99. Washington's Law Against Discrimination prohibits discrimination based on all of the following factors EXCEPT

   A. marital status.
   B. age.
   C. credit history or criminal background.
   D. use of a trained guide dog or service animal by a disabled person.

100. A person who believes that he or she has been illegally discriminated against may file a complaint with the Washington

   A. Board of REALTORS®.
   B. Attorney General.
   C. Real Estate Commission.
   D. Human Rights Commission.

101. If a discrimination complaint involves a real estate transaction, it must be filed with the State Human Rights Commission within

   A. 60 days after the alleged act.
   B. 3 months after the alleged act.
   C. one year after the alleged act.
   D. three years after the alleged act.

102. Under presumed buyer agency, if the licensee has entered into a written agreement with the seller, the licensee is the agent of the

   A. seller.
   B. both the buyer and the seller.
   C. neither the buyer nor the seller.
   D. buyer.

103. Two separate salespeople from the same brokerage wish to represent different parties to a transaction. In this situation,

   A. only one agent from a brokerage may be involved in a transaction at any given time.
   B. if this relationship is permitted, the broker has broken the law and is subject to fines, imprisonment, or both.
   C. each salesperson represents only the party with whom he or she has an agency relationship.
   D. both salespeople are presumed to represent both parties as dual agents.

104. A licensee listed W's house and served as a seller's agent. After the house is under contract, W wants to buy another house and wants to be represented by his listing agent. Can the listing agent now represent W?

   A. No, the licensee may only continue to represent W as a listing agent
   B. No, the licensee may not represent W because the listing agency relationship has been terminated
   C. Yes, the licensee may now represent W as a buyer's agent
   D. Yes, but the licensee must serve as a dual agent, representing W as a listing agent and a buyer's agent

105. The licensee must provide a pamphlet on the law of real estate agency to all parties to whom the licensee renders brokerage services when the party

   A. waives his or her rights.
   B. consents to dual agency.
   C. signs an offer in a real estate transaction handled by the licensee.
   D. performs any of the above.

106. In Washington, a dual agent owes the duty of loyalty to

    A. no party to the transaction.
    B. all parties to the transaction.
    C. the principal only.
    D. the broker.

107. In Washington, a licensee must keep confidential information concerning a principal confidential. However, some information must be disclosed. The licensee must disclose information that

    A. if disclosed, would operate to the detriment of the licensee's principal.
    B. relates to material facts about the property.
    C. the principal reasonably expects to be kept confidential.
    D. was acquired by the licensee during the course of an agency relationship with the principal.

108. Under the law of agency in Washington, the duty to disclose requires that the agent accomplish which of the following?

    A. Conduct an independent inspection of the property
    B. Conduct an independent investigation of the financial condition of the parties
    C. Independently verify the accuracy and completeness of any statements made by either party or other source
    D. Disclose any material defect in the property that is known by the agent

109. Under Washington law, a material fact is considered to be the fact or suspicion that the property, or neighboring property, is or was the site of

    A. a murder, suicide or other death.
    B. political or religious activity.
    C. illegal drug or gang-related activity.
    D. periodic flooding.

110. The agent represents the seller whose property was the site of a grisly murder. A prospective buyer asks the agent about the crime. The agent should

    A. deny the crime because it does not constitute a material fact.
    B. tell the prospective buyer the truth about the event.
    C. deny any knowledge of the crime so as not to hinder the transaction while not committing misrepresentation.
    D. tell the buyer to talk to the neighbors.

111. A crime committed on the property has affected the physical condition of the property. Information about the crime is

    A. not a material fact and disclosure constitutes a breach of duty to the principal.
    B. a material fact but cannot be disclosed.
    C. a material fact and must be disclosed.
    D. not a material fact, but should be disclosed anyway.

112. The agency pamphlet is designed to inform and educate the public concerning agency law. In a real estate transaction,

     A. the consumer may pick it up at any public library.
     B. the consumer may obtain it by writing to the Washington Real Estate Commission's Agency Review Board.
     C. the licensee must give it only to the principal with whom the licensee has an agency relationship.
     D. the licensee must give one to all parties to the transaction.

113. A broker may receive compensation from any of the following EXCEPT

     A. the seller.
     B. the buyer.
     C. a third party.
     D. a lender in return for referring the loan.

114. Most agency disclosure paragraphs also include

     A. the duties that the licensee agrees to accomplish.
     B. a statement that the party has received the Agency Pamphlet required by law,
     C. the amount of compensation to be received by the licensee.
     D. a list of things that the licensee will not be performing.

115. Washington agency statute defines liability for the harm caused by others as

     A. imputed liability.
     B. vicarious liability.
     C. mutual liability.
     D. liability of substitution.

116. With the advice and approval of the Commission, the Director of the Department of Licensing shall

     A. author the questions for the state portion of the real estate licensing examinations.
     B. issue rules and regulations to govern the activities of real estate licensees.
     C. investigate complaints to see if the Commission has jurisdiction.
     D. proctor the real estate exam held at least once per month.

117. The Director of the Department of Licensing is responsible for all of the following EXCEPT

     A. holding hearings.
     B. granting or denying licenses to real estate license applicants.
     C. setting the general real estate tax range for each county in the state of Washington.
     D. enforcing all laws, rules, and regulations relating to the licensing of real estate licensees.

118. The Director of the Department of Licensing has all of the following powers EXCEPT

     A. instituting a program of real estate education.
     B. imposing disciplinary sanctions.
     C. determining the amount of homestead exemption available to homeowners in the state of Washington.
     D. establishing standards of licensure for applicants licensed in other jurisdictions.

119. The legal advisor for the Director of the Department of Licensing is

   A. an attorney appointed by the Attorney General's office.
   B. an attorney appointed by the office of the District Attorney.
   C. the District Attorney.
   D. the Washington State Attorney General.

120. Which of the following acts in an advisory capacity to the Director of the Department of Licensing?

   A. The Real Estate Board
   B. The Washington Association of REALTORS®
   C. The Washington Real Estate Commission
   D. Educational Steering Committee

121. How many members serve on the Washington Real Estate Commission?

   A. 4
   B. 6
   C. 8
   D. 12

122. Members of the Washington Real Estate Commission are appointed for terms of

   A. 3 years.
   B. 4 years
   C. 5 years.
   D. 6 years.

123. Any vacancies on the Washington Real Estate Commission will be filled by

   A. appointment by the Director of the Department of Licensing.
   B. popular election.
   C. election by the existing members of the commission.
   D. appointment by the governor.

124. A real estate broker is an individual who

   A. lists or sells real estate for another for compensation.
   B. buys land, subdivides, and builds houses.
   C. offers advice on whether or not a project will make money.
   D. works under the supervision of a more qualified individual.

125. A real estate broker is a person who negotiates or offers to negotiate, either directly or indirectly, the purchase, sale, lease, or exchange of a

   A. business franchise that does not include any real estate.
   B. yacht.
   C. mobile home and the land on which it is located.
   D. cemetery lots.

126. A real estate broker is licensed to assist in the listing or selling of a

   A. manufactured home and the land on which it is located.
   B. houseboat.
   C. multi-level marketing plan.
   D. recreational vehicle.

127. Which of the following individuals is required to obtain a real estate license?

    A. Person who purchases property for his or her own purposes, or for a group of which he or she is a member
    B. Receiver, trustee, executor, administrator, guardian or person acting under court order, or seller under a deed of trust
    C. Person who buys or offers to buy real estate for another for a commission or other compensation
    D. Secretary, bookkeeper, accountant, or other office personnel who performs only clerical duties in a brokerage office

128. Which of the following individuals is required to obtain a real estate license?

    A. Manager of residential dwelling units on an incidental basis and not as his or her principal source of income
    B. Person who owns or manages a self-service storage facility
    C. Resident manager of a complex of residential dwelling units where the manager resides
    D. Anyone who buys or sells business opportunities for another for compensation

129. Which of the following tasks requires that a personal assistant working under the direct instructions and supervision of a licensee first obtains a real estate license?

    A. Submitting forms and changes to multiple listing services or obtaining status reports on loan progress and credit reports
    B. Serving as a courier delivering documents so long as he or she does not discuss or interpret the documents
    C. Greeting people at an open house or model unit and distributing preprinted promotional literature
    D. Answering questions and interpreting printed information concerning the property

130. A personal assistant working under the direct instructions and supervision of a licensee must hold a real estate license in order to

    A. show properties to prospective buyers.
    B. follow-up on loan commitments after a contract has been negotiated and pick up and deliver loan documents.
    C. write and place advertisements.
    D. obtain public information from sources like government offices, utility companies, and title companies.

131. Of the following, who can operate a real estate brokerage business and represent clients?

    A. A licensed salesperson
    B. A real estate broker
    C. A facilitator
    D. A mediator

132. Which of the following is a requirement for obtaining a broker's license?

    A. Successfully complete 120 hours of mandated instruction in real estate and pass the broker's license exam
    B. Pass the broker's license examination
    C. Maintain a permanent residence in the state of Washington
    D. Submit proof of brokering at least 125 transactions

133. All of the following may be used as an experience waiver in lieu of the required two years experience as a salesperson prior to obtaining a broker's license EXCEPT

    A. 5 years experience as a real property fee appraiser or salaried appraiser for a government agency.
    B. 5 years experience in development, financing, selling, and leasing of residences, apartments, or commercial buildings.
    C. 5 years experience in real estate investment, property management, or analysis of investments.
    D. having a finance degree with a minor in real estate.

134. Of the following, who can manage a branch office for his or her broker?

    A. Salesperson
    B. Broker's spouse or other blood relative
    C. Associate broker
    D. Employee hired for that purpose

135. A temporary broker's permit may be issued to a legally accredited representative of a deceased or incapacitated broker for a period not exceeding

    A. 30 days.
    B. four months.
    C. six months.
    D. one year.

136. In order to obtain a salesperson's license, an applicant must

    A. be 21 years of age or older.
    B. successfully complete 72 hours of instruction in real estate fundamentals.
    C. pass a salesperson's examination.
    D. complete an approved course within one year of application.

137. If an individual's license has been returned to the Director of Licensing for any reason, that individual's license becomes

    A. restricted.
    B. unrestricted.
    C. void.
    D. inactive.

138. A person with an inactive license

    A. may only engage in restricted real estate activities.
    B. is considered unlicensed and may not engage in real estate activities.
    C. may only engage in real estate activities under the direction of a licensed broker.
    D. must renew his or her license within 24 hours of any participation in a real estate transaction.

139. An inactive license may be placed on active status by

    A. petitioning the Washington Real Estate Commission.
    B. retaking the licensing examination.
    C. initiating a retrieval action in court.
    D. filling out an application and returning it to the Director of the Department of Licensing.

140. Laws and regulations relating to the denial, suspension, and revocation of a license

    A. are only applicable to active licenses.
    B. carry higher penalties for an active license than they do for an inactive license.
    C. are applicable to both active and inactive licenses alike.
    D. are applicable only to inactive licenses.

141. A land development representative may

    A. sell real estate.
    B. negotiate for the broker in an agreement relating to the sale of real estate.
    C. bind the broker in an agreement relating to the sale of real estate.
    D. distribute information and take prospects to the land site.

142. Which of the following is a requirement for an individual to be registered as a land development representative?

    A. Must be 21 years of age or older
    B. Furnish such proof as the director may require concerning the applicant's honesty and good reputation
    C. Complete a 30-hour course on land development
    D. Pass the land development representative examination

143. The real estate license examination tests the applicant on all of the following EXCEPT

    A. understanding of the principles of conveying real estate.
    B. understanding of Washington criminal law.
    C. appropriate knowledge of the English language, including reading, writing, spelling and math.
    D. purposes and legal effect of deeds, mortgages, land contracts of sale, exchanges, rental and option agreements, and leases.

144. When do real estate licenses issued to corporations, limited liability companies, limited liability partnerships, and partnerships expire?

    A. Two years from the date of issuance
    B. On the designated broker's second birthday following issuance of the license
    C. One year from the date of issuance
    D. They do not expire, but exist in perpetuity

145. A broker may establish branch offices under

    A. no more than two names.
    B. the name of the main office only.
    C. as many names as he/she wishes as long as the appropriate fees are paid for each name used.
    D. no more than three names.

146. A broker establishes a branch office. What must be included on any signs, advertisements, and letterhead for the branch office?

    A. Name of the main office
    B. Name of the branch office
    C. Both the name of the branch office and the name of the main office
    D. The name of the broker in charge of both the branch office and the main office

147. At a disciplinary hearing, all of the following may be represented by an attorney EXCEPT

    A. an administrative law judge.
    B. the department of licensing.
    C. the accused licensee.
    D. the person making the accusation.

148. If the accused licensee does not appear for his or her disciplinary hearing, the

    A. hearing must be rescheduled.
    B. licensee may be found in contempt of court.
    C. hearing will be held in his or her absence.
    D. licensee must pay a fine and the hearing will be rescheduled.

149. If the director finds that the accusation against a licensee is not proved by a fair preponderance of evidence, the

    A. licensee may sue the person making the accusation for defamation.
    B. director will notify the person making the accusation and ask if he or she is willing to drop the charges.
    C. director will order a more thorough investigation of the case.
    D. director will notify all parties and dismiss the case.

150. If the director finds that a licensee has violated the license law, the director can impose any of the following sanctions EXCEPT

    A. require that the licensee complete a course in the area of real estate practice relevant to the rule violated.
    B. order that the licensee be imprisoned for not more than 30 days for each offense.
    C. suspend, revoke, or deny the license.
    D. levy a fine not to exceed $1000 for each offence.

151. The director imposes a sanction against a licensee. When does the sanction order become effective?

    A. Immediately
    B. 10 days after the order is mailed to the licensee
    C. 30 days after the order is mailed to the licensee
    D. When it is filed

152. If the licensee wishes to appeal the decision made by the director in a disciplinary hearing, the appeal and bond must be filed within

    A. 48 hours of the director's decision.
    B. 7 days of the director's decision.
    C. 30 days of the director's decision.
    D. 60 days of the director's decision.

153. A transcript of the disciplinary hearing will be prepared at the licensee's expense, which will be delivered to the court hearing the appeal. If the licensee does not pay the cost of the transcript, the appeal will be dismissed. From the time that the transcript is filed, how many days does the licensee have to pay for the transcript?

    A. 10 working days
    B. 14 days
    C. 15 days
    D. 30 days

154. If the director makes a written finding of fact that the public interest will be irreparably harmed by delay in issuing an order, the director may issue a

    A. license revocation.
    B. denial of licensure.
    C. temporary cease and desist order.
    D. temporary restricted license.

155. The prosecuting attorney of each county will prosecute any violation of the license law that occurs in his or her county. If the prosecuting attorney fails to act, who may the director ask to take action in lieu of the prosecuting attorney?

    A. District attorney
    B. Attorney general
    C. Any attorney of the director's choosing
    D. County prosecutor

156. Disciplinary sanctions will be warranted if the broker accepts the services of, or continues to maintain in a representative capacity, any associate broker or salesperson who

    A. is under investigation.
    B. resides in a different county.
    C. is not receiving adequate compensation.
    D. is not licensed.

157. Disciplinary sanctions will be warranted if the licensee accepts something other than cash, or its equivalent, as earnest money without communicating that fact in writing to the owner before

    A. delivery of the offer to purchase.
    B. closing the transaction.
    C. acceptance of the offer to purchase.
    D. accepting this commodity as earnest money.

158. Disciplinary sanctions will result if the licensee commits any act of fraudulent or dishonest dealing or a crime involving moral turpitude. At a hearing, what is considered conclusive evidence of this?

    A. Findings of a state investigation
    B. Testimony of the principal or any other party to the transaction
    C. Certified copy of the final holding of any court of competent jurisdiction
    D. Investigation of a narcotics charge

159. Disciplinary sanctions will be warranted if the licensee accepts employment or compensation for appraisal of real property contingent upon reporting

    A. the actual value.
    B. a predetermined value.
    C. within a particular time range.
    D. an estimated value.

160. Disciplinary sanctions will be warranted if the licensee misrepresents his or her membership in any

    A. state or national real estate association.
    B. development company.
    C. brokerage firm.
    D. chamber of commerce.

161. Which of the following is a legal activity and will NOT warrant disciplinary sanctions?

    A. Depositing earnest money into the trust account
    B. Acting as a vehicle dealer without having a license to do so
    C. Violating an order to cease and desist issued by the director
    D. Any conduct in a real estate transaction which demonstrates bad faith, dishonesty, untrustworthiness, or incompetence

162. Disciplinary sanctions are warranted if the licensee fails to keep an account of escrow or trustee funds deposited with him/her relating to a real estate transaction for a period of

    A. 1 year.
    B. 3 years.
    C. 5 years.
    D. 7 years.

163. Disciplinary sanctions will be warranted if the licensee fails to furnish a copy of any listing, sale, lease, or other contract relevant to a real estate transaction to all signatories thereof

    A. prior to execution.
    B. within three days after execution.
    C. within 48 hours after execution.
    D. at the time of execution.

164. Disciplinary sanctions will be warranted if the licensee directs any transaction involving his or her principal to any lending institution or escrow company in expectation of receiving a kickback or rebate without first disclosing such expectation to

    A. his or her broker.
    B. his or her principal.
    C. all parties to the transaction.
    D. the lending institution in question.

165. Disciplinary sanctions will be warranted if the licensee buys, sells, or leases, either directly or through a third party, any interest in real property without disclosing in writing that he or she

    A. has bought, sold, or leased the property.
    B. does not represent any party to the transaction.
    C. represents one of the parties to the transaction.
    D. holds a real estate license.

166. Disciplinary sanctions will be warranted if a broker licensee fails to

    A. provide courses in real estate practice for all of his or her licensed associate brokers and salespersons.
    B. exercise adequate supervision over the activities of his or her licensed associate brokers and salespersons.
    C. maintain at least five licensed brokers in each of his or her branch offices.
    D. hire adequate licensed or unlicensed assistants to fully serve his or her clients and customers.

167. The director will suspend an individual's license for

    A. nonpayment or default on a federal or state-guaranteed educational loan or service-conditional scholarship.
    B. failure to pay child support.
    C. neither of these.
    D. either of these.

168. If an individual's license has been suspended for defaulting on an educational loan, that individual's license will be reissued when the director is provided with a written

    A. release from the lending agency stating that the loan has been forgiven.
    B. release from the lending agency stating that the person is making payments in accordance with a repayment agreement.
    C. statement from the individual consenting to pay the loan in full.
    D. release from the lending agency stating that the person has repaid the loan in full.

169. A broker will be held liable for the conduct of his or her affiliated licensee under which of the following circumstances?

    A. The salesperson violated a provision of the license law in contravention of the brokers specific written policies.
    B. The broker had taken reasonable measures to verify that adequate supervision was being performed.
    C. Upon learning of the violation, the broker attempted to prevent or mitigate the damage.
    D. The broker was aware of, but did not participate in the violation.

170. Every licensed real estate broker must maintain an office in Washington that is accessible to the

    A. director.
    B. broker's clients or customers.
    C. public.
    D. courts.

171. A broker is actively licensed in another jurisdiction. How long must the broker maintain trust account and transaction records in the state of Washington?

    A. 1 year
    B. 2 years
    C. 3 years
    D. 4 years

172. A broker who is actively licensed in another jurisdiction wants to be licensed in Washington. The applicant must provide the address of his or her out-of-state headquarters and

    A. where the broker intends to maintain his or her office in Washington.
    B. the names and addresses of each transaction performed in Washington.
    C. where his or her records are maintained in Washington.
    D. the names of each of the licensees affiliated with the broker.

173. A real estate broker wishes to maintain an office in a residential building. All of the following conditions must be met EXCEPT that the

    A. office must be separate from any living quarters.
    B. office must be identified as a real estate office by a sign at the office entrance that is visible to the public.
    C. office must be accessible to the public by a street address that can be reasonably located.
    D. broker must live on the premises.

174. The broker's license must be kept

    A. in a safe deposit box at a registered lending institution.
    B. in a file where the broker conducts business.
    C. prominently displayed in the broker's office.
    D. in the broker's place of residence.

175. If a licensee changes the location of his or her business, the licensee must

    A. first receive permission from the director to change his or her business location.
    B. notify the Department of Licensing of his or her change of address within 30 days.
    C. file a change of address with the Department of Licensing before transacting business at the new location.
    D. surrender the license to the director and a new one with the new address will be issued.

176. The relationship between a broker and a salesperson or associate broker may be terminated

    A. unilaterally by either the broker or the salesperson or associate broker.
    B. only by the employing broker.
    C. only with the written consent of the director.
    D. only by the salesperson or associate broker.

177. If the license of a salesperson or associate broker has been lost, an affidavit of lost license will have to be completed by

    A. a representative from the Department of Licensing.
    B. the broker.
    C. the salesperson or associate broker.
    D. both the broker and the salesperson or associate broker.

178. When a broker terminates a licensee's services for a violation of the license law,

    A. the broker must immediately file a written statement of the facts with the director.
    B. the broker's license will be immediately suspended or revoked.
    C. the licensee's real estate license will be immediately suspended or revoked.
    D. both the licensee's and the broker's licenses will be immediately suspended or revoked.

179. A branch office license is not necessary when all real estate sales activity is conducted on and limited to a particular subdivision or tract, as long as a licensed office is located within

    A. 5 miles of the subdivision or tract.
    B. 35 miles of the subdivision or tract.
    C. 50 miles of the subdivision or tract.
    D. 10 miles of the subdivision or tract.

180. Every licensee, within 20 days of service or knowledge thereof, must notify the real estate program manager of

    A. any criminal complaint, information, indictment, or conviction in which the licensee is named as a defendant.
    B. entry of a civil court order, verdict, or judgment against the licensee involving any real estate or business-related activity.
    C. neither of these.
    D. both of these.

181. The broker must deliver all documents signed by the parties, including earnest money receipts, listing agreements, and the closing statement

    A. within 24 hours of the time of signing.
    B. at the time of signing.
    C. within 5 business days of signing.
    D. within 14 days of the time of signing.

182. For each transaction, the broker must maintain a transaction folder containing all of the following EXCEPT

    A. deeds.
    B. agreements and documents.
    C. closing statements and correspondence.
    D. leases.

183. The source document for a lease must contain all of the following information EXCEPT

    A. the name and address of the tenant.
    B. the address of the leased premises, if different from the tenant's address.
    C. the square footage of the leased unit.
    D. the duration of the lease and the rental amount.

184. For sales transactions, a copy of the earnest money agreement, a copy of the final settlement statement, and any addenda related to the accounting or disposition of client funds must be

    A. maintained by a certified title company.
    B. kept at a separate location from the location where the trust bank account records are maintained.
    C. kept at the same location where the trust bank account records are maintained.
    D. kept at the main office or any branch where the broker is licensed.

185. For a corporate, limited liability company, limited liability partnership, or partnership license, prior to issuing a new license indicating a change of designated broker the licensee must submit

    A. a termination agreement from the outgoing designated broker.
    B. an application form from the incoming designated broker.
    C. a statement of the change of designated broker.
    D. evidence that the requirements have been satisfied.

186. Unless otherwise agreed to in writing, all checks received as earnest money, security or damage deposits, rent, lease payments, contract or mortgage payments on real property, or business opportunities owned by clients, must be made payable to the

    A. lessor.
    B. seller or escrow agent.
    C. real estate broker as licensed.
    D. client who owns the real property or business opportunity.

187. A legible copy of the agreement to purchase shall be retained in the files of the

    A. broker representing the seller.
    B. broker representing the buyer.
    C. broker who received a commission from the seller.
    D. participating real estate brokers.

188. An escrow agent wishes to close a real estate transaction and wants to charge a fee. In order to do this, the escrow agent is required to hold

    A. an escrow license.
    B. an office.
    C. an affiliation with a Title Company.
    D. a certificate of registration.

189. The closing statements of all transactions in which a real estate broker participates must show all of the following EXCEPT

    A. clear evidence of title.
    B. the date of closing.
    C. the total purchase price of the property.
    D. an itemization of all adjustments, money, or things of value received or paid and showing to whom each item is credited or debited.

190. A sales agreement has been negotiated by more than one broker, and the purchaser deposits funds prior to the closing. The broker who first receives the funds will keep them and be accountable for them until they are distributed in accordance with written instructions signed by

    A. all participating brokers.
    B. all parties to the transaction.
    C. all parties to the transaction and all participating brokers.
    D. the escrow agent.

191. Any amendment or modification to the property management agreement must be made in writing and signed by

    A. the owner.
    B. the owner and the broker.
    C. all tenants of the property, if residential.
    D. all tenants of the property whether residential or industrial.

192. A property management agreement, which must be written and signed before a broker can manage a property, must include all of the following EXCEPT

    A. a listing of tenant obligations.
    B. the broker's compensation.
    C. the type and number of individual units in the project or the square footage if the property is something other than residential.
    D. whether or not the broker is authorized to collect and disburse funds, and for what purpose.

193. The Shoreline Management Act regulates development within what distance of any high water mark?

    A. 100 feet
    B. 50 yards
    C. 200 feet
    D. 500 feet

194. The Washington Land Development Act applies to anyone selling or advertising how many unimproved lots to the public as part of a common promotional plan?

    A. 100 or more
    B. 50 or fewer
    C. 51 or more
    D. 26 or more

195. A developer does not provide the buyer with a public offering statement before the buyer signs a purchase contract. How many days after receiving the statement does the buyer have to rescind the contract?

    A. Two days
    B. 24 hours
    C. Five business days
    D. 30 days

196. Before receiving approval to develop land, the subdivision developer must comply with regulations concerning the size of the lots, the location of streets and sidewalks, the amount of open space, and the presence of adequate utilities. Of the following, which group gives approval to these plans?

    A. Owner's association
    B. Environmental Protection Agency
    C. Planning commission
    D. Lending institution.

197. What act requires an environmental impact statement (EIS) to be prepared in connection with all state and local government actions that may have a significant impact on the environment.

    A. Comprehensive Environmental Response, Compensation, and Liability Act
    B. Hazardous Waste Control Act
    C. State Environmental Policy Act
    D. Resource Conservation and Recovery Act

198. The State Environmental Policy Act and Shoreline Management Act laws are examples of whose authority?

    A. City
    B. County
    C. State
    D. Federal

199. In Washington, any property that is not separate and is acquired after marriage by either the husband, wife, or both is considered

    A. individual property.
    B. community property.
    C. property held in tenancy by the entirety.
    D. property held in joint tenancy with right of survivorship.

200. Under the Washington State theory of community property, both spouses are required to join in executing the security agreement or bill of sale for

    A. household goods.
    B. furnishings and appliances.
    C. a community mobile home.
    D. all of these.

201. Community real estate in Washington is subject to

    A. mechanics liens for labor and material furnished in erecting structures and improvements on the property.
    B. judgment liens for community debts.
    C. both mechanics liens and judgment liens.
    D. only mechanics liens.

202. Washington homestead protection is

    A. an equitable right.
    B. a statutory right.
    C. an inalienable right.
    D. a right of ownership.

203. If a homestead property is sold to satisfy the owner's debts, which of the following represents the first allocation from the proceeds of the sale?

    A. Amount of the homestead exemption is paid to the owner
    B. Amount of the debt is paid to the creditor
    C. Balance is paid to the owner
    D. Proceeds divided between the creditor and the owner

Answer Key

1. A. The broker earned the commission since the seller accepted the offer. The deposit must be returned to the buyer, and the broker cannot take his or her commission from it.

2. D. If both parties agree, then the brokerage can represent both parties. Agency is about representation; payment of fee does not determine representation.

3. B. Confidential information must remain confidential forever. The original agent no longer has an agency relationship with the seller and is now free to represent the buyer. The agent must disclose information about the physical condition of the property.

4. C. A licensee may have his or her license revoked or suspended if found guilty of directing any transaction involving his principal to any lending institution for financing in expectation of receiving a kickback or rebate without first disclosing such an expectation to his principal.

5. A. In the absence of a listing agreement, a licensee is presumed to represent the buyer, and that representation begins as soon as the licensee begins providing brokerage services. This can mean that as soon as a salesperson begins helping a prospective buyer, i.e., merely discussing housing needs with a prospect who attends an open house, that salesperson (and his or her broker) represents that buyer.

6. C. A licensee who performs real estate brokerage services for a buyer is a buyer's agent unless the licensee has entered into a written agency agreement with the seller, in which case the licensee is a seller's agent and can work with the buyer as a customer. There is no dual agency here, since the buyer does not want representation.

7. C. Each salesperson may represent only the party with whom he or she has an agency relationship. This is referred to as "split" or "designated" agency. In a transaction in which different licensees affiliated with the same broker represent different parties, the broker is a dual agent while each salesperson solely represents the party with whom he or she has an agency relationship, unless all parties agree in writing that both salespersons are dual agents. The broker must get both the buyer and seller to agree to this arrangement.

8. D. A licensee who performs real estate brokerage services for a buyer is a buyer's agent by statute. Payment for these services can come from any source without affecting the agency status. If one has a "buyer contract," the fee would be addressed there. In any real estate transaction, the broker's compensation may be paid by the seller, the buyer, a third party, or by sharing the compensation between brokers. RCW 18.86.080(7)

9. C. Information that relates to material facts about the property must be disclosed. One of the duties owed to a principal is the duty "not to disclose any confidential information from or about the principal." The statutory definition of confidential information supersedes the common law definition. Information received during the course of an agency relationship that the principal expects to be kept confidential and which, if disclosed, would be to the detriment of the principal, should not be disclosed.

10. B. The law was not created to confuse the public nor to create paperwork. Washington States agency law has four primary objectives: (1) to clarify and codify the common law of agency as it applies to real estate brokers and salespersons; (2) to create presumptions of agency relationships with consumers that are consistent with their natural expectations; (3) to reduce instances of dual agency, and (4) to eliminate vicarious liability and imputed knowledge as to consumers.

11. C. A broker may collect a commission from more than one party if both parties give their informed consent. In any real estate transaction, the broker's compensation may be paid by the seller, the buyer, a third party, or by sharing the compensation between brokers. An agreement to pay, or payment of compensation, does not establish an agency relationship.

12. D. Well before closing, the licensee must provide a pamphlet on the law of real estate to all parties to whom the licensee renders real estate brokerage services, regardless of whether the licensee is acting as an agent. This pamphlet must be provided before the party signs an agency agreement with the licensee, signs an offer in a real estate transaction handled by the licensee, consents to dual agency, or waives any rights, whichever occurs earliest. This duty may not be waived.

13. C. The disclosure statement is only a disclosure statement; it is not considered part of any written agreement between the buyer and seller. The buyer should recognize that it is neither a warranty nor a guaranty. Since the seller is making the disclosures, the licensee cannot be held liable for the contents of the disclosure statement, unless the licensee knew of a defect in the property and encouraged the seller not to disclose it.

14. C. The property disclosure law applies only to residential real property. Residential property is defined as (1) real property consisting of, or improved by, one to four dwelling units, (2) a residential condominium, unless the sale is subject to the public offering statement required in the Washington condominium act, or (3) a residential timeshare, unless subject to written disclosure under the Washington timeshare act.

15. D. The property disclosure law applies to one-to-four dwelling units; thus, the seller of a duplex must comply. The property disclosure law does not apply to a foreclosure, deed-in-lieu of foreclosure, or a sale by a lien holder who acquired the residential real property through foreclosure or deed-in-lieu of foreclosure.

16. C. The disclosure law applies to a sale to a friend or acquaintance of a transferor. The property disclosure law does not apply to a gift or other transfer to a parent, spouse, or child if that transfer is from a parent or spouse.

17. B. The disclosure statement must be delivered to the buyer no later than five business days after mutual acceptance of a written contract to purchase between a buyer and a seller. The parties can mutually agree on a different time frame if they desire.

18. C. Federal Fair Housing laws prohibit discussion of HIV or AIDS. "Psychological impacts" or "stigmas," such as a murder/suicide, are not considered material facts under Washington license law and therefore do not have to be disclosed. However, a licensee must respond truthfully if asked about such matters.

19. D. The salesperson does not have to resign but will have to inform the owner in writing that the salesperson is a licensee before making the offer.

20. A. Whether or not the licensee is a party's agent, the licensee owes to all parties to whom the licensee renders real estate brokerage services the disclosure of all existing material facts known by the licensee and not apparent or readily ascertainable to a party. This duty may not be waived.

21. D. The disclosure statement must be given before any offers are signed. The duties of a licensee include "to disclose in writing to all parties to whom the licensee renders real estate brokerage services, before the party signs an offer in a real estate transaction handled by the licensee, whether the licensee represents the buyer, the seller, both parties, or neither party."

22. C. The disclosure was a violation of license law. The licensee owes a duty of confidentiality to the tenant who hired the licensee. Payment of a fee does not determine representation.

23. B. The disclosure law does not apply to a transfer where a buyer had an ownership interest in the property within two years of the date of the transfer. Examples include an ownership interest as (1) a partner in a partnership, (2) a limited partner in a limited partnership, (3) a shareholder in a corporation, (4) a leasehold interest, or (5) transfers to and from a facilitator pursuant to a tax deferred exchange.

24. A. Split or designated agency occurs when two separate salespeople from the same brokerage represent different parties to a transaction. In a transaction in which different licensees affiliated with the same broker represent different parties, the broker is a dual agent, while each salesperson solely represents the party with whom he or she has an agency relationship, unless all parties agree in writing that both salespersons are dual agents.

25. C. The broker must disclose the cracked foundation as a material fact. The suicide is considered a "psychological impact" or "stigma" and is not considered a material fact and does not have to be disclosed. However, a licensee must respond truthfully if asked about such matters.

26. B. A licensee who performs real estate brokerage services for a buyer is a buyer's agent unless the licensee has entered into a sub agency agreement with the seller's agent, in which case the licensee is a seller's agent. Independent Multiple Listing Services in Washington have replaced the traditional offer of sub agency with an offer of "cooperation and compensation."

27. D. The broker must disclose to the purchaser at the first personal meeting that the broker represents the seller. A licensee owes all parties to whom the licensee renders real estate brokerage services the duty of providing a pamphlet on the law of real estate agency. This must be provided before the party signs an agency agreement with the licensee, signs an offer in a real estate transaction handled by the licensee, or consents to dual agency or waives any rights, whichever occurs first.

28. A. The dual agent can provide comparable market data to the seller after the buyer requests such data from the salesperson. The dual agent may not disclose any confidential information from or about either party, except under subpoena or court order, even after termination of the agency relationship.

29. C. A licensee rendering real estate brokerage services owes to all parties the following duty which may not be waived: disclosing in writing, before the party signs an offer in a real estate transaction handled by the licensee, whether the licensee represents the buyer, the seller, both parties, or neither party.

30. C. A licensee may act as a dual agent only with the written consent of both parties to the transaction.

31. D. The law does not require that the licensee conduct a property inspection. The duties of a licensee and the duties of the seller's agent under Chapter 18.86 RCW, Real Estate Brokerage Relationships, include the following: keep confidential information confidential, advise the consumer to seek expert advice for matters that are beyond the licensee's expertise (such as conducting a property inspection), and disclose all material facts known by the licensee.

32. B. The Washington State Department of Licensing administers the real estate license law. License law consists of laws passed by the state legislature and rules promulgated by the director of the Department of Licensing. All real estate licensees are required to obtain a copy of the license law, which is available from the Department of Licensing.

33. A. The governor appoints the six commission members for a term of six years each. At least two commission members must be from west of the Cascade mountain range and at least two must be from the east of the Cascade mountain range.

34. A. The director of the Department of Licensing has the authority to institute a program of real estate education. The Washington Real Estate Commission may hold educational conferences, administer the exams at testing sites, and prepare the real estate exam.

35. C. The license law consists of laws passed by the state legislature and rules promulgated by the director of the Department of Licensing. All real estate licensees are required to obtain a copy of the license law, which is available from the department of Licensing.

36. C. All license fees are paid to the state treasurer and placed in the real estate commission account in the state treasury. All money derived from fines imposed under the license law is deposited into the real estate education account.

37. B. When a license is issued to a corporation, limited liability company or limited liability partnership, one corporate officer, manager, or partner (who is named in the license application) may act as a real estate broker on behalf of the corporation, limited liability company, or limited liability partnership.

38. D. It is unlawful for any person to act as a real estate broker, associate real estate broker, or real estate salesperson without first obtaining a real estate license. Furthermore, no lawsuit can be brought to collect compensation as a real estate agent without proof that the real estate agent was duly licensed prior to offering to perform any real estate services.

39. A. An officer, partner, or manager must be designated as a broker before a license will be granted to a corporation, limited liability company, limited liability partnership, or partnership.

40. B. A real estate license is not required to sell a manufactured or mobile home. By definition, a mobile home is not real estate and thus is not engaging in the real estate business. If the sale of a manufactured or mobile home is made in conjunction with the purchase, sale, exchange, rental, or lease of the land upon which the manufactured or mobile home is or will be located, then a license is required.

41. B. A broker candidate must have a high school diploma or its equivalent, be at least 18 years of age, and have at least two years of experience as a salesperson prior to applying for the broker's license exam. No college is required.

42. D. A broker may establish one or more branch offices under a name or names different from that of the main office if the director approves the name or names, so long as each branch office is clearly identified as a branch or division of the main office.

43. D. A broker's license can be issued to an individual, corporation, or partnership, but not a trust.

44. A. A 30-hour trust account course can be used for the elective. The mandatory instruction must include thirty hours each of brokerage management, business management, and real estate law.

45. D. An applicant has five years to take the test after successfully completing an approved sixty clock-hour course in real estate fundamentals. In this example, October 31, 2006 would be the latest the person could apply for a salesperson's license.

46. B. If a broker applicant receives an experience waiver, and then fails to pass the broker's examination, the applicant loses the privilege of the waiver and must then satisfy the two-year experience requirement.

47. C. Post-secondary education with minor study in real estate for four years is not acceptable as experience to obtain the waiver. The applicant can ask for the waiver with five years experience as a real estate officer in a bank, title, or mortgage company, as a real estate attorney, or a real estate major plus one year experience as a real estate salesperson. All of these experience waivers must occur within the last seven years prior to the date of application for them to be valid waivers.

48. B. When the director receives a statement or accusation, the director will carry out a preliminary investigation of the facts to determine whether the statement or accusation warrants formal action. If it does, the director will set the matter for hearing at a specified time and place. The director may not give out a warning, nor wait to see if other accusations are received.

49. C. A copy of the order setting the time and place of a disciplinary hearing and a copy of the verified statement of accusation against the licensee will be given to the licensee at least twenty days before the day of the hearing.

50. C. The director or an Administrative Law Judge will conduct the hearing. Attorneys can represent the Department of Licensing, the licensee, and the person making the accusation.

51. A. The director is not required to initiate any of the suggested actions but according to statue the director may impose any one or more of the following sanctions: suspend or revoke licenses, deny applications for licenses, fine violators or require the completion of a course in a selected aspect of real estate practice relevant to the provision of the rule violated.

52. C. When filing an appeal, the licensee must post a $500 bond with the court clerk. The appeal and bond must be filed within thirty days of the director's decision.

53. A. Any violation of the license law is a gross misdemeanor and can be prosecuted by the county prosecutor or by the state attorney general.

54. B. The director may issue a cease and desist order to a person after notice and hearing and a determination that the person has violated a provision of the License Law or a lawful order or rule of the director.

55. C. When a temporary cease and desist order is served, the hearing to determine whether the order will become permanent must be held within thirty days after the department receives the request for hearing, unless the licensee requests a later date.

56. B. Continuing to sell any real estate whereby the interests of the public are endangered, after the director has, by order in writing, stated objections, would warrant disciplinary sanctions.

57. C. Advertising by a licensee without including the broker's name as licensed will warrant disciplinary sanctions. If a real estate licensee is advertising his or her personal real property, the licensee need disclose only that he or she holds a real estate license.

58. A. If a corporation that has been incorporated in another state applies for a real estate license, the applicant must furnish a certified copy of certificate of authority to conduct business in the state of Washington. It must also furnish a list of its officers and directors and their addresses and evidence of current registration with the Secretary of State. There is no need to provide information regarding the license number of its salespeople or proof of real estate activity.

59. B. To take the real estate exam, the applicant must apply on the proscribed form and pay the license exam fee. The applicant must also provide proof of honesty, truthfulness, and good reputation, as well as identity, which may include fingerprints. A parent's signature is not required.

60. A. Examination results are valid for one year only. Anyone who has passed the license examination must become licensed within one year from the date of the exam. Otherwise, the applicant must take and pass another exam before he or she can be licensed.

61. C. The license application must be signed by the broker or designated broker to whom the license will be issued. The branch manager may sign for the broker or designated broker for licenses that are to be issued to that branch office.

62. A. A minimum score of 70% on each portion of the real estate salesperson examination is required to pass. Applicants for the broker license must receive 75%.

63. B. Persons who have been convicted of a crime within ten years of application may be required to submit fingerprint identification on a form provided by the department of real estate prior to issuance of a license.

64. A. The completed license application form serves as an interim license that is effective for up to 45 days – by which time the licensee's permanent license should have arrived. The postmark date of the application, or date of hand delivery to the licensing division, is the date the interim license becomes effective.

65. D. The salesperson who just sent in her application may receive an interim license. There are no interim licenses for designated brokers for corporations, limited liability companies, partnerships, limited liability partnerships, individual real estate brokers, or associate brokers.

66. B. Every real estate license expires on the applicant's second birthday following issuance of the license. Licenses issued to corporations, limited liability companies, limited liability partnerships, and partnerships expire two years from the date of issuance. The date of issuance becomes the renewal date.

67. D. Licenses must be renewed every two years on or before the expiration date and a biennial license renewal fee must be paid. The director will issue license and pocket identification to each active licensee.

68. B. If a year has passed since the expiration date, the license will be cancelled. If the license is applied for within a year of the renewal date, the individual will have to pay a penalty.

69. A. All real estate licensees must successfully complete a total of thirty clock-hours of instruction every two years in approved real estate courses in order to renew their licenses. The exception is during the first renewal period: the salesperson must successfully complete a thirty clock-hour course in real estate practices and pass a course examination approved by the director.

70. C. Up to fifteen clock hours of instruction beyond the required thirty hours in two years may be carried forward for credit in a subsequent two-year period. To count towards this requirement, a course must be started within thirty-six months before the proof date for renewal.

71. D. Commission rates are always negotiable between the seller and the broker. Grounds for revoking a broker's license include a felony conviction, false advertising, and commingling of funds.

72. D. Conversion of any money, contract, deed, note, or mortgage to his or her personal use shall be prima facie evidence for revoking the salesperson's license.

73. B. Depositing earnest money into the firms escrow account is legal. Grounds for disciplinary action include misrepresentation, performing work without a required license, and advertising without the broker's name.

74. B. A licensee may place a "For Sale" sign in front of a house with the permission of the seller.

75. C. A broker who assists the buyer in falsifying a loan application for the purposes of obtaining a larger loan can lose his or her license and be fined. Any conduct in a real estate transaction, which demonstrates bad faith, dishonesty, untrustworthiness, or incompetence is subject to discipline by the Director of Licensing.

76. D. All advertising must be done in the name of the broker. J-H must also include her broker's name.

77. A. If someone relies on the licensee's misrepresentation, to the person's detriment, the licensee will be subject to disciplinary sanctions.

78. C. Advertising real property in any manner without including the broker's name is a violation.

79. B. A licensee advertising his or her personally owned real property must only disclose that he or she holds a real estate license.

80. B. Failure to return monies or documents held in trust within 30 days of a demand for their return may be considered a conversion of such money or documents and will warrant disciplinary sanctions.

81. A. A salesperson's website must include the licensee's name and the firm's name as registered in the jurisdictions in which he or she holds licenses. Washington state guidelines for advertising and procuring prospects on the internet, adopted September, 2000, have provided standards for online practice by licensee and licensed firms to enhance online real estate consumer protection. These standards include "Licensee" and "Licensed Firm" disclosure.

82. C. A broker or salesperson should not post other broker's listings without written permission. If permission is given, the broker or salesperson should not alter the online display or any informational part of the listing without written permission from the listing broker.

83. B. A license is required to answer questions and interpret printed information concerning the property. According to the Washington Real Estate Commission, a personal assistant who works under the direct instruction and supervision of a licensee may be unlicensed if he or she greets people at an open house or model unit, performs clerical duties, or submits forms and changes to the MLS.

84. D. Commissions are always negotiable between the principal and the agent.

85. A. Commissions are always negotiable between the principal and the agent. A broker may not pay commissions and/or referral fees to an unlicensed person.

86. D. All funds or moneys received on behalf of his or her principal must be deposited in the broker's real estate trust bank account no later than the first day following receipt of the funds.

87. B. A broker shall maintain a pooled, interest-bearing trust account identified as a "housing trust fund account" for deposit of trust funds that are ten thousand dollars or less. The interest from this account is remitted to the state treasurer and is divided as follows: 75 percent to the housing trust fund and 25 percent to the real estate education account.

88. D. A broker shall maintain a pooled interest bearing trust account identified as housing trust fund account for deposit of trust funds that are ten thousand dollars or less.

89. B. The real estate broker is responsible for the custody, safety, and correctness of the entries of all required real estate records. The broker retains this responsibility even though another person may be assigned the duties of preparation, custody, or recording of the records.

90. C. A broker is not required to maintain a duplicate cash receipts journal kept in a safe deposit box. For automated systems, the separate ledger sheets may be a computer- generated printout, which contains required entrees.

91. B. The broker is required to keep pre-numbered checks with the check register and cash disbursements journal or check stubs. The broker must keep validated duplicate bank deposit slips. Reconciled statements must also be retained.

92. A. The broker must keep a duplicate receipt book or a cash receipts journal recording all receipts and validated duplicate bank deposit slips.

93. D. The broker does not keep copies of deeds. The broker must keep a transaction folder containing all agreements, contracts, documents, leases, closing statements, and correspondence for each transaction, and for each rental, lease, contract, or mortgage collection account.

94. D. It is an unfair practice to use the sex, race, creed, color, national origin, marital status, or the presence of any disability to determine the credit worthiness of an applicant for credit, including a real estate loan.

95. A. The Law Against Discrimination is administered by the Washington State Human Rights Commission. It is composed of five members who are appointed by the governor with the advice and consent of the senate. Its task is to formulate policies and make recommendations to government agencies. It also hears complaints about alleged violations of the law.

96. D. The Seller must complete the disclosure form in its entirety to the best of his or her knowledge. No space is to be left blank. If the seller doesn't know the answer to the question, he or she should answer, "don't know." If the question clearly does not apply to the property, the seller is to write "N/A"

97. C. Unless otherwise agreed to, the buyer may exercise one of two options within three business days of receipt of the real property transfer disclosure statement: (1) approve and accept the real property disclosure statement, or (2) rescind the agreement for the purchase and sale of the property.

98. B. If the buyer does not deliver a written rescission notice to the seller within the three-day period, or as otherwise agreed to, the real property transfer disclosure statement is deemed approved and accepted by the buyer.

99. C. Those persons with credit problems or a criminal background are not considered a protected class in Washington. In addition to the federally protected classes of race, color, religion, national origin, sex, families with children, and presence of any sensory, mental, or physical disability, Washington's Law Against Discrimination prohibits discrimination because of marital status, age, or the use of a trained guide dog or service animal by a disabled person.

100. D. The Law Against Discrimination is administered by the Washington State Human Rights Commission. It is composed of five members who are appointed by the governor with the advice and consent of the senate. Its task is to formulate policies, make recommendations to government agencies, and hear complaints about alleged violations of the law.

101. C. Complaints alleging an unfair practice in real estate must be filed with the Human Rights Commission within one year after the alleged action. Discrimination complaints not related to real estate must be filed with the commission within six months after the alleged act of discrimination. Any person who claims to have been discriminated against may file a written complaint with the Human Rights Commission. The commission may also issue a complaint on its own motion.

102. A. A licensee who has entered into a written agency agreement with the seller represents this person as a seller's agent.

103. C. Each salesperson represents only the party with whom he or she has an agency relationship. This is referred to as "split" or "designated" agency. In this transaction the broker is a dual agent, while each salesperson solely represents the party with whom he or she has an agency relationship, unless all parties agree in writing that both salespersons are dual agents.

104. C. The licensee may now represent W as a buyer's agent. Agency relationships are transaction specific, i.e., the authority and duties of the agent are limited to the specific transaction. A licensee may work with the same party in separate transactions with different relationships.

105. D. This pamphlet must be provided to all parties to whom the licensee renders real estate brokerage services before the parties sign an agency agreement with the licensee, signs an offer in a real estate transaction handled by the licensee, consent to dual agency, or waive any rights, whichever occurs earliest. This duty may not be waived.

106. A. A dual agent is not bound by loyalty to either party in the transaction. Rather than stating that a dual agent has the duty of loyalty, a dual agent is required only to refrain from taking action that is adverse or detrimental to either party's interest in a transaction.

107. B. A licensee must always disclose information relating to material facts about the property. Washington State now has a statutory definition of confidential information that supersedes the common law definition. Such confidential information can include any information that if disclosed, would operate to the detriment of the licensee's principal, any information that the principal expected to remain confidential, and any confidential information that was acquired in a previous agency relationship.

108. D. A licensee must always disclose any known material defect in the property. Unless otherwise agreed, a licensee is NOT obligated to conduct an independent inspection of the property, an independent investigation of either party's financial condition, or independently verify the accuracy or completeness of any statement made by either party.

109. D. It is considered material that the area is prone to flooding and this must be disclosed. The fact or suspicion that the property, or any neighboring property, is or was the site of a murder, suicide or other death, rape or other sex crime, assault or other violent crime, robbery or burglary, illegal drug activity, gang-related activity, or political or religious activity stigmatizes a property. Since these do not affect the physical condition of, or title to, the property, they are not considered material facts.

110. B. While the seller's agent is not obligated to disclose the murder to prospective buyers, if the prospective buyer asks the agent about the crime, the agent cannot lie. The agent must answer the prospect's questions honestly.

111. C. If a crime does affect the physical condition of the property, it is a material fact. For example, if the property was used to manufacture illegal drugs, this fact must be disclosed because there could be chemical residue left on the property that could endanger the buyer.

112. D. The agency pamphlet that must be given to all parties in the transaction is a brochure designed to inform and educate the public about agency law. The cover page is a summary of Washington's agency statute and refers the reader to specific sections of the statute. The body of the pamphlet itself is the complete text of the agency statute.

113. D. The lender may not "kickback" a fee in return for referring the loan. In any real estate transaction, the broker's compensation may be paid by the seller, the buyer, a third party, or by sharing the compensation between brokers. A seller may agree that a seller's agent may share the compensation with another broker. A buyer may agree that a buyer's agent may share the compensation with another broker.

114. B. Most agency disclosure paragraphs also include a statement that the party has received the Agency Pamphlet required by law.

115. B. Vicarious liability is a liability for the harm caused by others. The provisions in Washington agency statue regarding vicarious liability are a substantial departure from common law. Until 1997, a principal could have been liable for the harm caused by his or her real estate agent or sub-agents of that agent. Today, a principal is not liable for an act, error, or omission by his or her agent or sub-agent.

116. B. With the advice and approval of the Commission, the Director of the Department of Licensing shall issue rules and regulations to govern the activities of real estate licensees.

117. C. The director is NOT responsible for setting the general real estate tax range for each county of the state. The director is responsible for holding hearings, granting or not granting licenses, and enforcing rules and regulations relating to real estate licensees.

118. C. The director is NOT responsible for determining the amount of homestead exemption available to homeowners in the state of Washington. The director has all the other powers listed here.

119. D. The Washington State Attorney General is the director's legal advisor. The director may appoint an adequate staff to assist him or her. Neither the director nor any employees can be involved in any real estate business.

120. C. The Washington Real Estate Commission acts in an advisory capacity to the director. It meets at least four times a year and is authorized to hold educational conferences for the benefit of the industry and to prepare and administer the real estate exam.

121. B. The Washington Real Estate Commission consists of six members appointed for terms of six years each. Each commission member must have at least five years experience in the sale, operation, or management of real estate in the state of Washington. Alternatively, each must have at least three years experience in investigative work of a similar nature, preferably in connection with the administration of Washington real estate license law.

122. D. Members of the Washington Real Estate Commission are appointed for terms of six years each.

123. D. The governor may fill any vacancies on the commission for the unexpired term.

124. A. A real estate broker is defined as a person who sells or offers for sale, lists or offers to list, buys or offers to buy real estate or business opportunities or any interest therein, while acting for another for commissions or other compensation or the promise thereof.

125. C. A real estate broker is defined as a person who negotiates or offers to negotiate, either directly or indirectly, the purchase, sale, exchange, lease, or rental of real estate or business opportunities or of manufactured or mobile homes and the land on which they are located. Dealing with cemetery lots in Washington does not require a real estate license.

126. A. A real estate broker is licensed to assist in the listing or selling of a manufactured home and the land on which it is located.

127. C. Any person who buys or offers to buy real estate for another for a commission or other compensation must hold a real estate license. Individuals buying for their own purposes, court appointed persons, and office clerical personnel are exempt from the licensing requirements.

128. D. Any person who buys or sells business opportunities for another for compensation must have a real estate license. The other individuals listed here are exempt from the licensing requirements. RCW 18.85.010 (1)(a) defines "business opportunity" as including business, business opportunity, good will of an existing business, or any one or combination thereof.

129. D. The Washington Real Estate Commission requires that a personal assistant be licensed in order to answer questions and interpret printed information concerning the property. A personal assistant who works under the direct instructions and supervision of a licensee may be unlicensed and submit forms and changes to the MLS, act as a courier delivering documents, and greet people at an open house.

130. A. A personal assistant is required to have a real estate license to show property to prospective buyers. According to the real estate commission, an unlicensed personal assistant who works under the direct instruction and supervision of a licensee may follow up on loan commitments, write and place advertisements, and obtain public information.

131. B. Only a broker can operate a real estate brokerage business and represent clients.

132. A. A candidate applying for a broker's license must pass the broker's license examination and successfully complete 120 hours of mandated instruction. It is not necessary to maintain a permanent residence in the state of Washington in order to obtain a broker's license or submit proof of 125 transactions.

133. D. A finance degree with a minor in real estate will not qualify as a waiver. Applicants for a real estate broker license who do not possess two years of actual experience as a full-time real estate salesperson may write a letter requesting approval of alternative qualifications or experience and indicating the basis for such a request. Alternative qualifications or qualification by reason of practical experience in a business allied with or related to real estate could include five years experience as a fee appraiser, a developer, real estate investor, property manager, or investment analyst.

134. C. An associate broker can manage a branch office for his or her broker.

135. B. In the case of a deceased or incapacitated broker, a temporary broker's permit may be issued for four months. The purpose of the temporary permit is to allow the "temporary broker" to complete any pending transactions.

136. C. An applicant for a salesperson's license must pass a salesperson's exam, be eighteen years of age or older, and successfully complete a sixty-hour course, approved by the director, in real estate fundamentals. This course must be completed within five years prior to applying to take the salesperson's license examination.

137. D. An inactive license is one that has been delivered (returned) to the director for any reason. For example, when a salesperson quits working for a particular broker, the broker must deliver that salesperson's license to the director, which is then placed on inactive status. When the salesperson chooses a new broker to work for, the salesperson's license is placed back on active status and sent to the new broker.

138. B. A person with an inactive license is considered unlicensed and may not engage in real estate activities.

139. D. An inactive license may be placed on active status by filling out an application and returning it to the director. If a license is inactive for more than three years, the licensee must successfully complete a thirty-clock hour course in real estate within one year of applying for active status.

140. C. Laws and regulations relating to the denial, suspension, and revocation of a license are applicable to both active and inactive licenses alike.

141. D. The land development representative is restricted to disseminating information, contacting prospective purchasers, and transporting prospective purchasers to the land site. They may not engage in any real estate conduct or activity such as selling, negotiating, receiving or handling funds, or assisting in the preparation of documentation directly involved in the sale of real estate.

142. B. The minimum requirements for an individual to be registered as a land development representative are that the applicant must be eighteen years of age or older, furnish such proof as the director may require concerning the applicant's honesty and good reputation, and provide identification which may include fingerprints. There is no requirement for a course or an examination.

143. B. The real estate exam does NOT test on an understanding of Washington criminal law. It does test on the principles of real estate, appropriate knowledge of English, including math, and the purpose and legal effect of deeds, mortgages, land contracts, etc.

144. A. Licenses issued to corporations, limited liability companies, limited liability partnerships, and partnerships expire two years from the date of issuance. The date of issuance will be the future renewal date.

145. D. No broker may establish branch offices under more than three names. Both the name of the branch office and the name of the main office must clearly appear on any signs, advertisements, letterhead, etc. of the branch office.

146. C. Both the name of the branch office and the name of the main office must appear on any signs, advertisements, letterhead, etc, of the branch office. No broker may establish branch offices under more than three names.

147. A. The director or an administrative law judge will conduct the hearing and thus will not be represented by an attorney. Attorneys can be present to represent the department of licensing, the licensee, and the person making the accusation.

148. C. The hearing will be held and a certified transcript will be made of the proceedings. The licensee is entitled to a copy of the transcript, at the licensee's expense.

149. D. If the director finds that the accusation against a licensee is not proved by a fair preponderance of evidence, the director will notify all parties and dismiss the case.

150. B. If the director finds a violation of the license law, the director may not order imprisonment. The director can suspend, revoke, or deny a license, levy a fine not to exceed $1000 for each offense, or require the completion of a course in a selected area of real estate practice relevant to the section of the chapter or rule violated.

151. B. If the director imposes a sanction against a licensee, a copy of the sanction order will be filed and a copy will be mailed to the licensee. The order becomes effective 10 days after mailing.

152. C. When filing an appeal, the licensee must post a $500 bond with the court clerk. The appeal and bond must be filed within 30 days of the director's decision.

153. C. A transcript of the disciplinary hearing will be prepared at the licensee's expense, which will be delivered to the court hearing the appeal. The licensee is notified when the transcript is filed and has 15 days to pay for the transcript. If the cost of the transcript is not paid within 15 days, the appeal will be dismissed.

154. C. The director may issue a temporary cease and desist order. Whenever possible, the director will give notice by telephone or otherwise of the proposal to issue the order before issuing the temporary cease and desist order.

155. B. The director may ask the attorney general to take action in lieu of the county prosecuting attorney.

156. D. A broker may be disciplined if he or she accepts the services of, or continues to maintain in a representative capacity, any associate broker or salesperson who is not licensed.

157. C. To avoid disciplinary sanctions, before the offer to purchase is accepted, the licensee must communicate in writing to the owner that something other than cash, or its equivalent, is being offered as earnest money.

158. C. A certified copy of the final holding of any court of competent jurisdiction in such a matter is considered conclusive evidence in any hearing under the license law chapter. Disciplinary sanctions will result for committing any act of fraudulent or dishonest dealing or a crime involving moral turpitude.

159. B. Accepting employment or compensation for appraisal of real property contingent upon reporting a predetermined value will warrant disciplinary sanctions.

160. A. Misrepresentation of a licensee's membership in any state or national real estate association will warrant disciplinary sanctions.

161. A. Depositing earnest money into the trust account is proper and will not warrant a disciplinary action. Disciplinary sanctions are warranted if acting as a vehicle dealer without a license, violating a cease and desist order, or any conduct which demonstrates bad faith, dishonesty, untrustworthiness, or incompetence.

162. B. In a real estate transaction, failing to preserve records for at least three years following its consummation will warrant disciplinary sanctions. The account must show to whom the funds are paid and other pertinent information as the director may require.

163. D. At the time of execution, failing to furnish a copy of any listing, sale, lease, or other contract to all signatories of a real estate transaction will warrant disciplinary sanctions.

164. B. The licensee must first disclose any such expectation for a kickback or rebate to his or her principal. Failure to do so will warrant disciplinary sanctions.

165. D. A licensee must always disclose in writing that he or she is buying, selling, or leasing directly, or through a third party, any interest in real property. Failure to do so will warrant disciplinary sanctions.

166. B. A broker licensee's failure to exercise adequate supervision over the activities of his or her licensed associate brokers and salespersons will warrant disciplinary sanctions. The broker licensee is not expected to provide real estate courses, hire personal assistants, or hire a specified number of associate brokers or salespeople.

167. D. A license can be suspended for failing to pay child support. The director will also suspend the license of anyone who has been certified by a lending agency and reported to the director for nonpayment or default on a federally or state-guaranteed educational loan or service-conditional scholarship.

168. B. Prior to the suspension, the agency must provide the person an opportunity for a brief hearing and issue a finding of nonpayment or default. The person's license will not be reissued until the person provides the director with a written release issued by the lending agency stating that the person is making payments on the loan in accordance with a repayment agreement approved by the lending agency.

169. D. A broker will be held liable for the conduct of his or her affiliated licensee if the broker was aware of, but did not participate in, the violation. A broker will not be held responsible for inadequate supervision if the broker has reasonable policies and procedures in place, and attempted to prevent or mitigate the damage.

170. C. Every licensed real estate broker must maintain an office in Washington that is accessible to the public.

171. C. The broker must maintain records in one location for three years. The location must be the office of one of the following: an escrow agent licensed in the state of Washington, a real estate broker licensed in the state of Washington, an attorney at law licensed to practice in the state of Washington, or a title company used for all Washington transactions for the broker.

172. C. A broker actively licensed in another jurisdiction who wants to be licensed in Washington must notify the department of the address where the records are maintained and must also include the address of the broker's out-of-state headquarters.

173. D. A real estate broker may maintain an office in a residential building provided that the office is separate from any living quarters, the office is identified as a real estate office by a sign at the office entrance that is visible to the public, the office is in conformance with existing zoning, and the office is accessible to the public by a street address that can be reasonably located.

174. C. The broker's license must be prominently displayed in the broker's office.

175. D. Written notice must be given to the director if any licensee changes the location of his or her business or branch office. The licensee's real estate license must be surrendered to the director and a new one with the new address will be issued.

176. A. Either the broker, salesperson, or associate broker may terminate the relationship unilaterally. The broker must give immediate notice of the termination to the director. The notice must be accompanied by the salesperson's or associate broker's license. Once the license is surrendered, the licensee ceases to represent the broker, and the license will become inactive.

177. D. If the license has been lost, both the salesperson or associate broker and the broker will have to complete an affidavit of lost license.

178. A. When the broker terminates a licensee's services for a violation of the license law, the broker must immediately file a written statement of the facts with the director.

179. B. A branch office license is not necessary when all real estate sales activity is conducted on and limited to a particular subdivision or tract, as long as a licensed office is located within thirty-five miles of the subdivision or tract.

180. D. Every licensee must, within twenty days after service or knowledge thereof, notify the real estate program manager of any criminal complaint, information, indictment, or conviction (including a plea of guilty or nolo contendere) in which the licensee is named as a defendant, or any entry of a civil court order, verdict, or judgment against the licensee in any court of competent jurisdiction in which the subject matter therein involves any real estate or business-related activity by the licensee. Notification is required regardless of any pending appeal.

181. B. Every real estate broker must deliver to all parties, at the time of signing, copies of all earnest money receipts, listing agreements, and all other similar documents signed by the parties, including the closing statement.

182. A. The broker is not required to maintain copies of deeds in the transaction folder. The transaction folder must contain all agreements, contracts, documents, leases, closing statements, and correspondence for each transaction and for each rental, lease, contract, or mortgage collection account.

183. C. The square footage of the leased unit is not required in the source document. The source document for a lease must contain the name and address of the tenant, the address of the leased premises if different from the tenant's address, the duration of the lease, the rental amount, the amount(s) of any and all deposits made by the tenant and the purpose of said deposits, the location where the deposits are being held, and any modification of the terms of the original lease document.

184. C. For sales transactions, a copy of the earnest money agreement, a copy of the final settlement statement, and any addenda related to the accounting or disposition of client funds must be kept at the same location where the trust bank account records are maintained.

185. D. Prior to issuing a new license indicating a change of designated broker for a corporate, limited liability company, limited liability partnership, or partnership licensee, the licensee must submit evidence that the requirements have been satisfied.

186. C. All checks received as earnest money, security or damage deposits, rent, lease payments, contract or mortgage payments on real property, or business opportunities owned by clients must be made payable to the real estate broker as licensed, unless it is mutually agreed upon in writing that the deposit will be paid to the lessor, the seller, or an escrow agent named in the agreement.

187. D. A legible copy of the agreement to purchase shall be retained in each participating real estate broker's file.

188. D. An escrow agent's certificate of registration is required in order to close a real estate transaction for compensation.

189. A. There is no requirement on the closing statement for clear evidence of title. The dates of the adjustments will be shown, together with the names of the payees, makers, and assignees of all notes paid, made, or assumed.

190. B. The written instructions to distribute funds must be signed by all parties to the transaction. The broker is not a party to the transaction.

191. B. Any amendment or modification to the property management agreement must be done in writing, signed by the owner and the broker, and kept on file. The tenants are not parties to a management agreement.

192. A. The property management agreement will not include a listing of tenant obligations. The agreement must include the broker's compensation, the type and number of individual units in the project or the square footage if the property is something other than residential, whether or not the broker is authorized to collect and disburse funds and for what purpose, authorization, if any, to hold security deposits and the manner in which security deposits may be disbursed, and the timeframe for furnishing summary statements to the owner.

193. C. The purpose of the Shoreline Management Act is to protect shorelines by regulating development within 200 feet of any high water mark. It applies to coastal shorelines, the shores of lakes larger than 20 acres, and the shores of streams flowing at a rate of more than 20 cubic feet per second.

194. D. The Washington Land Development Act applies to anyone selling or advertising 26 or more unimproved lots to the public as part of a common promotional plan, regardless of where those lots are located. In other words, even if the lots are located in another state, they are covered by this act if they are promoted in Washington.

195. A. The developer must give a public offering statement to each buyer before the buyer signs a purchase contract. Otherwise, the buyer can rescind the contract within two days after receiving the statement. If no statement is received, the buyer can sue the developer for damages.

196. C. The subdivision developer must submit plans regarding lot sizes, street locations, open space, and adequate utilities to the Planning Commission which then decides whether or not to approve the plan.

197. C. The State Environmental Policy Act (SEPA) is patterned after the National Environmental Policy Act (NEPA). It requires an environmental impact statement to be prepared in connection with all state and local government actions that may have a significant impact on the environment. SEPA also applies to any private developments that require the approval of the state, county, or city. This includes any actions that require rezones, conditional use permits, variances, or building permits.

198. C. The State of Washington created both of these laws.

199. B. Any property that is not separate and is acquired after marriage by either husband, wife, or both is community property.

200. D. Neither spouse can create a security interest, other than a purchase money security interest, in community household goods, furnishings, appliances, or a community mobile home unless the other spouse joins in executing the security agreement or bill of sale.

201. C. Community real estate is subject to both Mechanic and Judgment liens.

202. B. Homestead protection is a statutory right and all the provisions of the homestead law must be complied with before protection is granted. Homestead laws protect residences from being sold to pay off certain kinds of debts. This protection is fairly limited and never prevents the foreclosure of a mortgage loan.

203. A. If the property is sold, the proceeds of the sale are applied in the following order: (1) the amount of the homestead exemption will be paid to the homestead owner, (2) the amount of the debt will be paid to the creditor, and (3) any balance will be paid to the homestead owner.